Homecoming

Homecoming

POEMS

VICTOR CONTOSKI

© Victor Contoski 2000
First Edition
Library of Congress Control Number: 00-105591
ISBN: 0-89823-210-4
Book design and typesetting by Percolator
Cover: *Farmer's Wife II* by Wieslawa B. Contoski. Courtesy Victor Contoski
Printed in Canada

New Rivers Press is a nonprofit literary press dedicated to publishing emerging writers.

This activity is made possible in part by a grant provided by the Minnesota State Arts Board, through an appropriation by the Minnesota State Legislature. In addition, this activity is supported in part by a grant from the National Endowment for the Arts.

Additional support has been provided by the Kansas University Endowment Association Scholarly Publications Revolving Fund, the General Mills Foundation, the McKnight Foundation, and the contributing members of New Rivers Press.

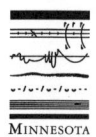

New Rivers Press
420 North Fifth Street Suite 1180
Minneapolis, MN 55401
www.newriverspress.org

For Dzidka

Contents

Part i. Temptations

3   The Wolves of My Childhood
4   Unhappy Couple
5   Hitting My Thumb with a Hammer
6   Cardinals
7   Temptations
8   A Note from a Friend
9   The Dance
10 The Dying Man
11 Dead Man's Dog
12 Cards in the Trash
13 The Turning
14 Conversation over Hot Coffee
15 Incriminating Evidence
16 My Wrongs
17 The Liar
19 Forgiveness
20 January
21 Social History of a Deck of Cards
22 Magicians
26 American Suite

Part ii. Fugues

33 Calendar Clock
34 Touch
35 At the Dry Well
38 South Wind
39 The First Time
40 The Last Time
41 Countdown
42 Tourists
43 Chess Players
44 Old Book
46 My Mistakes
47 Andromeda
48 Fugue in D Minor

Part III. The Uninvited

- 59 Spirit
- 60 Wherever I Turn
- 61 Frost
- 62 Sunset
- 63 A Death in the Family
- 64 Hunting Tricholomas
- 65 The Stone at the Top of My Head
- 66 Driftwood
- 67 Wisdom Teeth
- 68 Grandmasters
- 69 The Cry
- 70 Autumn House
- 71 My Father's Ties
- 72 Bridge
- 73 Rain after Drought
- 74 The Things of the Dead
- 75 Angels of Defeat
- 76 Sleeping Again in My Parents' House
- 77 First Snow
- 78 Quantrill's Raid
- 84 The Uninvited

Part IV. Lullabies

- 87 Music
- 88 A Dream of Old Classmates
- 90 Lament for Water
- 92 Gravel at the Window
- 93 End of a Winter Evening
- 94 Lullaby
- 95 Oranges
- 97 Memory
- 98 Dream Elegy
- 99 Unknown Insects
- 100 Gutters
- 101 Biology
- 102 Keys
- 103 Visitation
- 104 June

105 Argo
106 Homecoming
107 Somewhere Else
108 Black Stones
109 White Stones
111 Far Galaxy
112 Beyond Virgo
113 Lamps
114 A Day in Autumn

115 Acknowledgments

Part I.
Temptations

The Wolves of My Childhood

First they blew down
my houses of straw and wood
then my houses of brick and steel.

Now they strap me
to the operating table
and sharpen their instruments.

Under their surgical masks
I can hear them
huffing and puffing.

"Breathe deeply," they say
as the gas mask comes down
over my nose, my mouth,
and the hairs of my chinny chin chin.

Unhappy Couple

They came
like Magi

bearing between them
a box in a velvet cloth.

Among shepherds and oxen
they knelt in silk mantles.

We offer you the unhappiness
we have made between us
like a child.

It is all we have.
We want you to share it.

Hitting My Thumb with a Hammer

Uhh—and into the mouth.
Blood on the tongue
over the nail's horizon.
The thumb turns black
from cursing.

Alone in the middle of the room
the hammer hangs its head.

Nails smirk
in garages.

Fingers point and flail
like children
when their father collapses.

And as long as it lives
the thumb will remember
the kiss of flesh and steel
the hammer's hickey.

Cardinals

She spoke of cardinals
white teeth flashing
dark hair over dark eyes

how she longed to see
red bodies flying
and black masked faces
against the snow

Now she has taken a lover
and moved away.

All morning
the red flags of cardinals
unfurl in the box elder tree.

Temptations

There they go
scurrying away
on all their hairy legs

down down
into their dark dens.

Quick!
After them!

Drink this, we tell them
pouring down our white poison.

Up they come
writhing drunkenly
carrying their horrid brown eggs
their children their children
as if they were dancing.

Then the music stops.

We poke them with sticks
and leave

to find next morning
the bird of song
in all the colors of the rainbow
dead at our feet.

A Note from a Friend

for Ed Rube

Your note folded its wings and settled
over the papers on my desk
hatching its eggs

mumbling its song
a cross between *ye-eah*
howaboutthat
and *cuckoo*.

All day it watches
over my world
like a bureaucrat
staring out the window
and dreaming of his pension.

The Dance

A sign over the dance hall reads
Go Tommies—win, win, win!
The team has just lost
the homecoming game
by thirty-six points.

Suits and ties
formal evening gowns
step together carefully
at arm's length.

The band
composed of last year's seniors
plays "The Blue Skirt Waltz"
as if it were a march.

The Dying Man

Color him red.
Put a red circle
around his house
with its shuttered windows

with its empty garbage cans
standing in front
like eye sockets.

Color his wife yellow
as she goes to work each day
her mouth a thin line
her eyes straight ahead.

Her head bobs to friends
as if something deep down
keeps tugging at it.

Color his children gray
as they board their school bus
as they raise their hands in class
as they eat lunch in silence.

Color his dog black
as it comes bounding
wagging its tail
sniffing your shoes
straining at the leash
held by the dying man.

Dead Man's Dog

The black dog of the dead man
comes rushing out of the morning mist

dragging the widow
on a leash.

Cards in the Trash

for two young girls molested by their fathers

The wind plays with them now
turning them over one by one

        pages of a book
        the fairy tales you grew up on
                the kind gray councillor
                the little girl who befriended animals
                      who jumped with joy
                playing
                        old maid
                        crazy eights
                        hearts . . .

    torn leaves
    commuters
            huddled against a viaduct
            waiting for the last train
                  into winter.

Read 'em and weep:
        sevens and eights of the workday
        old jacks
                waiting for their inheritance
        tattered kings and queens

    aces you thought
    were just waiting
    to hold your hand.

The Turning

She turned away
in slow motion
her shoulders folded.

And the day straightened up
      turned
      staggered
and went down for the count.

Conversation over Hot Coffee

Sit, down, he says.
Let's talk.

Before I can say a word
he turns
teeth clenched, arms flailing.
It's you. It's your fault.
Look what you've done.

And the scalding mess
of his life
comes pouring down
into my lap.

Incriminating Evidence

The words dismissed
with a careless wave
have come back scarred
covered with grime
after years on the road
guns in their belts.
We only did what you told us.

And numbers appear nightly
on the battlements
like the ghost of a murdered king.
He did it He's the one.

My Wrongs

Their powder flavors my food,
their antifreeze my drink.

They have sent the woman I love
a robe of fire
and murdered my unborn children.

I see them now
at the edge of the clearing
knives in their dirty hands
waiting for darkness.

The Liar

1
I give you my word.
He lied in his teeth
in his front teeth and his back teeth
in his crowns and his roots and his gum sockets
in his incisors and canines
his bicuspids and molars with their gold fillings
and in all the spaces in between.

He lied in his wisdom teeth
lying crooked in his gums.

He lied in his gums.

He lied in his tongue
in the front of his tongue
and the back of his tongue
in the taste buds at its sides
and in the soft underside.

He lied in his uvula.

He lied in his jawbone
and the hinges of his jaw.

He lied in his beard
in the short hairs
and in the long hairs
in the sideburns
and in the chin hairs.

He lied in the hairs in his nose.

He lied in his lips
that he puts to the lips
of those he loves.

He lied in his mouth
in the floor of his mouth
and the roof of his mouth

in his upper palate
and his lower palate.

He lied in his throat.

In the air he breathed in
and the air he breathed out
he lied.

2
Like the rubber band
a farmer places around
the testicles of his ram
so they will shrivel
and drop off

may these words
wind around his balls.

Forgiveness

Outside the rain falls
           like mercy
and from the kitchen
comes the smell of my old favorite
cream of hatred soup.

January

Once again the wind
nuzzling about the house
fingering the windows

whining

like an impotent man
who has bought a woman
for the night

and wants
his money's worth.

Social History of a Deck of Cards

1
In the beginning
the king was alone.

No suits. No colors.
Then the deuce came

and others masked
facedown on the table

2
At midnight they reveal themselves:
various fours eights and nines

the lumpenproletariat
sprawling on their backs
among crumpled money

while the owners push back chairs
and wander out into the night
where pistol barrels shine

like great black holes
between the stars of their teeth

Magicians

(Poetry Writers)

1
She cuts the world
with a razor blade
revealing the egg inside.

She cracks the egg
and peels it
revealing an eye.

Now she comes toward you.
You kneel down.
She puts the eye on your tongue.

2
Come, he says smiling
pulling his goatee
*I will show you your heart
under a shell.*

Watch closely!—he looks
into your eyes and you
cannot tear away
cannot even watch his hands
as they shift the shells.

Choose one, he commands
and you gesture blindly.

That's right, he says
lifting the shells,
*under each and every one—
your heart.*

3
I am changing my name to Sorrow.

When you see me turning somersaults
when you see me vanishing
        to thunderous applause
you will think I am happy.

But grief has turned my world
upside down.

4
The rich and the powerful
the oppressors of the world
have fashioned a great lumbering cart
and call it The Law.

Hitch yourself to the cart.

Here is the wand Justice.
Put it in your teeth and pull.

5
The sex goddess laughs and laughs.
Soon everyone laughs with her.

This is a sex goddess?

6
A magician rises and bows.

Gentleman be seated
ladies if you please

a volunteer from the audience
thank you kindly.

Two peas
ladies and gentlemen
two peas
> examine them
> observe them closely

> > one hard green crinkled
> > > the natural pea
> > the other crinkled painted black
> > > the artificial pea.

The magician turns his back.

> > Choose one
> > show it to the audience.
> > Place it here in this little vial.

The magician takes the vial

> > a few mystical passes
> > a few magic words

> > > *abracadabra*
> > > *abracadabra — kazoo!*

puts it behind his back
and takes out the false top.

Hold out your hand
> brave volunteer from the audience
and I will tell you

> > > *abracadabra — kazoo!*

that you chose the *natural pea*
the *natural pea*

as he tilts the vial
and pours into the astonished hand

> > water

7
The gentle one
sits in the corner.

You turn to him and
—oops! There he goes
off into infinity again
riding his tricycle
to the moon.

American Suite

PRELUDE

New York City
early dawn.

The bums in the Bowery
stagger toward morning
girls in the sweatshops
bow their heads
and bag ladies stir
in doorways and stone stairwells.

After a night of love
the New York Stock Exchange
rises at the bell
in monogrammed pajamas.

On the other side of the bed
Corporate Debt rolls over.
"Is it time already?"
She opens on eye.
"My hair is a mess."

In downtown Manhattan
the tall buildings
of Rockefeller Plaza
stand like bars

of music.

ALLEMANDE

The sun rises over the Hudson River
over the estate of Nelson Rockefeller.

The statues on the lawn
rise and stretch
sending their shadows west
toward the great mansion
where Degas and Renoir
where the Master of the Bimbo Triptych
and Rembrandt and Picasso
and the ghosts
of Nelson and Happy Rockefeller
sleep in curtained rooms
secure as tax shelters.

The maids
up and about in short skirts
dust Calder mobiles.

The butler
waits with breakfast
on a silver tray
(Italian, c. 1450).

And lo
the ghost of Nelson Rockefeller
rises from his Max Ernst bed.

Scratching his stomach
he moves sleepily
toward the bathroom
and Claes Oldenburg's
soft toilet.

Courante

David Rockefeller comes out
of the David Rockefeller wing
for a quick round of golf
with Andrew Jackson by Clark Mills
and Horatio Greenough's George Washington.

The Greek Slave by Hiram Powers
stands off to one side
loaded with golf bags.

The maids in their short skirts
come running through the sculptures
come running barefoot through the lawn
laughing and giggling
through the Cubis and Bronco Busters
through the George Washingtons
and Andrew Jacksons
and Greek Slaves
and the men servants after them.

They catch each other
and begin to make love.

David Rockefeller says softly,
"May I play through?"

Sarabande

Around noon Grief
a four-ton chunk of marble
arrives in a huge truck
to be lifted by winches
slowly carefully
and settled in a corner
of the well-manicured front lawn.

And the ghost of Nelson Rockefeller
wishes the well-manicured front lawn
were the big toe on the left foot
of Gerald R. Ford.

Gigue

And in the evening
champagne and laughter
guests in tuxedos and evening dresses
in Mercedes and Rolls-Royces.

A chamber orchestra
plays Bach's Suite in B Minor.

More champagne
more laughter.

Servants bring out sparklers
and the sons and daughters of the rich
take them into the dusk
among the great oaks and elms
among monuments of stone and steel
they drift laughing

like Christmas tree ornaments
like mobiles.

"Where's Happy?"

"She was here a minute ago."

Sparklers rush off
searching for her.

"Happy, Happy, where are you?"
"Come out, come out, wherever you are."

George Washington and Andrew Jackson
look on in stony silence.

The sparklers burn down.
They go out.

And then the headlights
of the Mercedes and Rolls-Royces
disappear into the night
with the Rockefellers
as a last guest calls out
to the Hudson River Valley,
"Happy? Happy?"

Coda

On the well-manicured front lawn
the moon rises silently
over Grief.

Part II.

Fugues

Calendar Clock

Music sounds
somewhere in the distance
a dead tenor
singing "Spirto Gentile."

The wind in the leaves
applauds and applauds.

Photographs of our parents
in their youth
line the walls of our home
like sheet music

and regular as a metronome
the old calendar clock
we bought at auction years ago
tells little by little
the truth.

Touch

for the pianist Mieczyslaw Horszowski

The legs go
>off on their own
>starting the long journey
>in small weak steps

>taking the body
>where it longs to go.

Strands of gray hair
follow them in silence

The back goes
>curved.

Hearing goes
taste goes
smell goes.

And the fingers go
>dancing dancing

>>remembering
>>>the rhythm the melody

>>the intricate figures
>>the dreams of youth

>>the touch
>>>of the other hand.

At the Dry Well

1
Life churns
        in the primal sea
        of a newly formed planet

Little by little
land appears.

Then something crawls
        little by little
out of the sea

for a cool drink of water.

2
Something almost human
slinks out of the forest
out onto the broad savannas
standing upright
        from time to time

as it stalks
a great-horned elk

on its way
to a cool drink of water.

3
Icarus
        soaring toward the sun
        on his wax wings
               thirsts

for a cool drink of water.

4
In the Hanging Gardens of Babylon
elegant Queen Amytis
asks her husband
> his hair grown like eagle's feathers
> his nails like claws
> his body wet
>> with the dew of heaven

for a cool drink of water.

5
at the marriage feast at Cana
Jesus solemnly turns water into wine
and wonders if he has forgotten something.

Later
> on the cross
> he remembers.

6
In a Renaissance garden
Simon Boccanegra
> Doge of Genoa
finds his long-lost daughter.

Back in his palace
on a side table
also waiting to be discovered
> poison

in a cool drink of water.

7
On the planet Barsoom
the last ruler
looks out glassy-eyed
over the dead sea bottoms
   where once
      the white sails of ships
      bellied out in the wind.

8
Your hand
   touches my forehead
    my eyes
    my lips.

At the dry well
   the cold aluminum cup
   of the dipper.

South Wind

All night long
a steady whisper

and snow
has been melting
in darkness.

The First Time

The first time
drops by unexpectedly
as if for a chat
or a cup of coffee

so natural
we almost don't recognize . . .

and then it is gone
and we are alone
jingling the change in our pockets
and whistling the song we learned
for the first time.

The Last Time

Years later
we meet again
hands trembling
hair gone gray
faces wrinkled.

"Long ago . . ."
"Didn't we . . . ?"
"Why . . ."

Our eyes meet
and we touch
for the last time.

Countdown

The countdown begins
for the long walk into autumn.

Cornbread and acorn squash
hum half-forgotten
songs from childhood.

Cold rain
touches our skins
like a soft drum.

Nestled at the feet
of sweetgums and sugar maples
jack-o-lanterns
lick their lips and cackle:
    Happy birthday
    Happy birthday.

And the hunter's moon
offers each and every one of us

a bag of poisoned candy.

Tourists

This is what we came to see:

    Arcturus
        in the west
        like a road sign

    Scorpio
        knocking its red belly
        on the neighbor's roof

    Ophiuchus
        in procession
        carrying his jeweled snake

    the Milky Way
        smeared
        all over the big top

a fat thumb of a moon

and Aquarius
        loping along
        poking his long nose
            into the night
        swinging Saturn
        in a bucket of stars.

Chess Players

Wherever we go
clocks tick
men and women sink
into themselves

An old master
sits as if asleep.

No one speaks.
No one breathes.

And pieces of wood
move in the silence
as if to music.

Old Book

I've been too long away from that book.
Time to read it again.

Go through those dog-eared pages looking
at my friends in their old fashions.

But they are different,
the chapters mixed.

Sally is older.
I can't find the young lieutenant
        and where is the jolly life in the greenwood?

A long time I walked behind my friend
and didn't recognize him, not at all
        he was so wasted
        unshaven
        the light gone out of his eyes.

Something is wrong here
—as if I were reading it backward.

I remember
        she married the orphan
        and the Duke recovered his inheritance
            but not here.
            It's all wrong.

I remember.

Here it's the Duke who dies in Africa
        wasted
        unshaven
        the light gone out of his eyes.

There's my friend. I'd know him anywhere.
There were marshmallows
and Father and Mother and Uncle Bob.

But the book is a different color.
The pages are torn.
Nobody respects it anymore.

Where has the lieutenant gone?

It's the wrong book, I say,
       for I remember
       I remember.

Yet here and there I find
drops of blood
brown and brittle as the pages.

It's my blood
that I used long ago
for a bookmark.

My Mistakes

Dawn.
The sun like a bugle-reveille.

And here they come
all my eager mistakes
rushing into formation.

The Officer of the Day
ramrod straight
presents them.

Swagger stick in hand
I ask for volunteers.

Hut! Hut! Hut!
All of them step forward.

I smile thinly.

Okay men.
This is it.
Follow me over the top.

Andromeda

Autumn cracks into names:
>*Alpheratz*
>*Mirach*
>*Almach*.

Crickets and cicadas
crank up
the prayer wheel of night

and all things turn
the living and the dead

the body of the one you love
sleeping beside you

the bones of your ancestors
the ghosts of the stars

monsters and heroes
distressed princesses
palaces and labyrinths.

Cetus turns.
Perseus turns away
      looking into his shield.
The head of Medusa turns.

Andromeda turns
chained to her stone
by the sea.

And M31
the Great Spiral Galaxy
like a lens
turns

Fugue in D Minor

for Girl, Torturer, and Broken Machine

CONTRAPUNCTUS I

1
It is early spring.
The cornfields are brown.
Beside the road is a patch of snow.
The refusal to melt is holy.

2
You have killed your best friend
in your dream. The blood
on the knife is holy.

3
The torturer has come for you.
His hands are soft as a woman's.
The compassion in his eyes is holy.

4
You are about to open a door
and enter a room full of harmony
where a beautiful girl is waiting.
You stop. The knob that will not turn
in your hand is holy.

5
The machine is busted.
Let it stand in the field and rust.
Rust is holy.

CONTRAPUNCTUS II

1
Between March and April
the snow by the road
and the brown cornfields

> *with a hey and a ho*
> *and a hey nonino . . .*

2
Your best friend lives!
Sunlight turns the knife
into a jewel.
The pattern on its handle
shifts
        sways
                pulses
like a song.

3
Ding dong!
        The torturer comes.
Give him your fingers
        so he won't take your thumbs.
Give him a dollar to go away.
Eeny, meeny, miney, mo.
Out go you.

4
A beautiful girl
listens to music
in another room.

Da-dum-de-dum
da-dum-de-de-dum.

Her feet   begin
        to move
she is dancing.

She turns.
She twirls.

She dances through the door . . .
        And into your arms.

5
The machine in the field

    sways

        it walks

            it dances—

Qrrkssb! Qrrkssb!

It joins you
    and the girl
    and your best friend
    and the torturer
and together you skip down the road
by the fields and the snow

    with a hey and a ho
    and a hey nonino

    Ding dong!

    Da-dum-de-dum
    da-dum-de-de-dum

    Qrrkssb! Qrrkssb!

CONTRAPUNCTUS III

1
Snow   stands
by   the   road
by   the   brown cornfields.

Spring
will never come.

2
Blood on the knife!

Like

      a patch of rust

      from the heart

      of your best friend

whom you killed

      in a dream

      from which

      you will never wake.

3
The eyes of the torturer
are like the eyes
of a young girl
who has just found
someone to love:
      it
      is you.

4
The door
is locked.
Behind it you
hear music playing
and picture a girl

dreaming

looking

out the window

waiting

for someone

to come

through the door

which will never open.

5
A holy rust

        covers

                the broken machine

like a blanket
over its face

as

        the metal stands
        in the field

            waiting

for a mechanic

        who will never come.

Contrapunctus IV

1
Snow holds on to the side of the road
with both hands. Tight. Hard.

It kicks. It bawls. It screams.
It has lost its voice through terror
but its mouth is still open and working.

The cornfields brace their feet
against the foothills—and push.

They put their shoulders to the snow
and heave and grunt and budge it
little by little, forcing it screaming
and kicking out onto the road,
out onto its long journey
into the silence.

2
Agh!
The blood on your hands sticks like sweat
as you wake screaming from your nightmare.

Your bed is a strewn battlefield
hot like a knife.

The floor under your bare feet
    is cold
like the body of your best friend
    and silent.

3
The torturer's hand pulls the lever.
The wheels of his machinery groan.
They twist. They writhe. They scream
    AAIEEHHK! AAIIEEHHK!

Higher and higher
like a whistling tea kettle.

The torturer trembles. He sweats.
He clenches his teeth.
    AAIEEHHK! AAIEEHHK!
The wheels wheeze. They grind. They cough.
Blood covers them like rust.

The torturer's hand turns white upon the lever.
He tries to push it up. It sticks.

    AAIEEHHK! AAIEEHHK!
    cries the machine

writhing in agony
spitting coughing up
the steel of its lungs.

     URG. URG.
     XL.

Then nothing.

The torturer
puts his head in his hands
and weeps

into the silence.

4
A girl wrings her hands.
She puts them over her ears.

The phonograph
its arm gone haywire
digs the needle deep into the record
like a torturer.
     Aawrng . . . aawwrrng . . . xl
The girl looks about wildly
searching for someone
to save her from dissonance.

You put your shoulder to the locked door
and heave. The frame shudders. Heave!
It shudders again. Heave!—and it splinters
with the sound of bone
in the hands of a torturer.
The phonograph stops screaming
but the wood of the door
still hangs on its hinges
like a dead man on a rope
who will not let you pass.

The record spins on
in silence

5
Through the broken door
you see a rusty machine
crawl through the window
pick up the girl
and leave

lumbering off down the road
with the girl in its coils

EEEeeeee!

You cannot tell
if the girl is screaming
or the machine needs oil.

EEEeeeee! EEEeeeee!
Then softer.
Eeee eeee . . . ee . . .

Then
silence.

CONTRAPUNCTUS V

The cornfields stand brown

like blood
on the hands of a torturer

like the eyes
of a beautiful girl
listening to music

like rust.

CONTRAPUNCTUS VI

1
Early spring.
Cornfields.

Snow by the road.
Though the weather is evil
the road is holy.

2
Dream of your best
friend killed by the knife in your hand.
Though the weapon is evil,
the dream is holy.

3
Torturer:
though the one he serves is evil
his eyes are holy.

4
A shattered door
bars you
from a beautiful girl.
Though the wood is evil
the space between you is holy.

5
A broken machine stands in the field.
Whatever evil has been done is paid for.

The machine rusts into silence.
And silence is holy.

Part III.
The Uninvited

Spirit

Spirit of joy
gentle one
opener of doors

when we first felt your claws
that day in the meadow
we thought they were pain.

Later as we sat reading
              each alone
         suddenly you were there
                  among the ghosts of the past
        among the galaxies
                  blazing on the page.

When we lay down
    your head
    rested on the pillow.

We see you now
only with our eyes closed.

We touch you
only in dreams.

Gentle one
spirit of joy

open once again
the door.

Wherever I Turn

Cats and books
scraps of paper

wherever I turn
in the world

your face.

Frost

1
All night
the steady thrupping
of an icy rain.

In gray morning
a thin layer of ice
where a cold hand
has touched the grass.

2
During the night
a black car with no lights
smashed into the mailbox
scattering its limbs
all over the driveway.

Someone has entered our house
while we slept
come into our bedroom
and turned off the night light.

Sunset

Since long before the white man
rode out onto the prairies
the sun has been going down.

A towering cottonwood sways in the breeze
rocking rocking the cradle in its branches.

The hero's eyes turn glassy.
His hand waves vaguely
toward something in his breast
as his knees buckle.

The giant coming down the beanstalk
feels it start to sway beneath him.

He looks down and sees Jack
with a silly grin and a hatchet
looming suddenly larger and larger

as the sun over Kansas
goes down and down and out.

A Death in the Family

The March wind
brings news from the south.

Seeds in their black loam beds
turn over in their sleep.

St. Stanislaus Polish school
in Winona Minnesota
erases its blackboards
and covers its mirrors.

The snow in the gullies
goes to confession
for the last time.

Fenceposts line up
and count off into infinity.

And light flutters down
over the fields
in Red Wing and Wabasha counties
      like a tablecloth.

Hunting Tricholomas

The gray one
    called the meeting
    away from tapped phones
    and curious eyes.

Soapy
    a cigarette in his lips
    runs a comb
    through his greasy hair.

Some in masks
    rehearse for the grand jury.
    "We don't know nothing.
    What ring? Never heard of it.
    Leave us alone, okay?"

The redhead
    has been around the block
    more than once.
    Look at her
    strut her stuff.

Three strip
    nonchalantly
    and lie in the sun
    their young bodies glistening.

The leopard
    leans against a pine tree
    making little kissing noise
    as he pats the .38
    in his shoulder holster.

In the distance
people appear
hunting mushrooms.

The Stone at the Top of My Head

Whenever I stand up
I bump my head
on a black stone.

I turn to the right
      it follows.
I turn to the left
      it follows
            hanging.

My white hair turns black
my eyes turn black
my tongue turns black.

You cannot live here
      not here
you have no space
you are heavy
you are blind,

A stone pushes you down
a black stone.

Driftwood

There they go
floating downstream
like the Lady of Shalott.

Knights fight to gain control of their mounts
as the current bears them deeper and deeper.

Bishops raise their eyes toward heaven
and pray silently with wooden lips.

Pawns
scattered leaves
drift facedown.

The queen spits blood.
Her water-soaked ermine robe
       heavy as guilt
pulls her body down.

The king feels his crown pushing
his head under
       time and again
like a giant thumb

as he bobs his way
toward the Isle of Avalon.

Wisdom Teeth

X rays show them
lying deep in my gums
at unnatural angles

deformed children
sleeping in the womb

who will never know
the dark cave
of the mouth
the teeth of day.

Crooked dice
thrown once and never again
they dream the dreams
of the unborn.

Grandmasters

On page after page of the old magazines
they sit before their boards gathering dust
      heads in their hands
        as if in mourning
            for broken treaties
            troop movements
            loved ones
                  fallen by the wayside.

A thin white film
like the pulverized monuments
of a forgotten civilization

falls over the boards
      over the pieces
      over the players

and still the dead sit
lost in thought.

The Cry

Suddenly wide awake.
What was *that?*

My hand goes out
        to find your body
        rowing steadily beside me.

Light answers my fingers:
        my slippers like sentries
        cats curled on the sofa
        books tucked snugly
                into their harbors
        records waiting in silence
                for their cues
        like the good food
                dormant in the icebox
        and the new day
                waiting in darkness.

Outside
        cardinals and robins
                fast in their nighttime perches
        Orion and his beasts
                steadfast in the sky
        with the moon like a faithful companion.

Back in bed
I touch your body
and close my eyes
        blessing with sleep
        whatever it was
        that cried out
        in love or pain.

Autumn House

The autumn wind
plays Vivaldi
on elm and cottonwood
sweetgum and maple.

Horses race
in the far field.

Our newly painted house
shines with honey.

Mushrooms bubble on the stove

and the yellow day
fades with the leaves

as we sit and eat.

My Father's Ties

Each morning
my fingers remember

> arranging the bills in my wallet
> adjusting the knots on my throat

my fingers

> without a sound
> over a cloth keyboard

> music for a deaf man

each morning in my fingers
as they place his ties
over my heart.

Bridge

for Uncle Fran

The living
study their hands.

Someone bends over slowly
his cards flutter down
and he falls.

Uncle father husband
he does not move.

One calls the ambulance.
Others pick him up carefully
carefully lay him on the couch.

Doctors appear
shaking their heads.

Life systems go on
and then go off.

What remains
goes to science.

Then one by one
we pick up memories
scattered like cards

aces and kings

shuffle them
cut
and deal.

Rain after Drought

When I wake
autumn

you beside me asleep
your hand on my arm

and a cold rain
knocking our house
with its tiny fists.

The Things of the Dead

Bison deer and cave bear
jumbled on one another
over the walls at Lascaux

the magic dead stand
pregnant on our walls
looking at the camera
pierced with our arrows.

The fruit of their trees
waits at the table.

In the keys of their typewriters
we touch their fingertips.

Their canes support us.
Their clocks chime
the hours of our lives.

Angels of Defeat

Bloated
they lurch home
on their dark wings

my upside-down children
the heavy black holes
in my heart.

Sleeping Again in My Parents' House

Awake suddenly
I open the hall door

and an old man
his face caked with clay
is swaying up the stairs
toward my parents' bedroom

and I am crying
Grandpa! Grandpa!

First Snow

The snow that fell
during the night
has melted everywhere
but on the road.

A cold white line
shows me the way
out of the world.

Quantrill's Raid

(to the music of Charles Hoag)

PASTORALE

Early morning August 1863
birds twittering before dawn
quail marching silently
out of the brush like soldiers.

Blue dawn
green day
the wheat in the fields . . .

Guns asleep in the armory . . .
People waking, rising, washing . . .

Lawrence flat and open
like the pages of summer
like the pages of history
into which men came riding four abreast . . .

BALLAD

Gather round you good people
I'll sing of Quantrill
and his band of bold brigands
come to burn and to kill.

Snug in their homes
people slept the night through.
Snug in the armory
their weapons slept too.

Unarmed Union recruits
just risen at dawn
were shot down in their tracks
and the slaughter was on.

It was first down Rhode Island;
where men stood they fell.
Then it's up Massachusetts
to the Eldridge Hotel.

Street by street, house by house,
raiders went through the town
taking men, taking boys
and shooting them down.

Then it's back to Missouri
back into the past
leaving widows and orphans
bodies and ash.

THE WOMEN

What can we say?

Four abreast men rode into town
rowdying and shooting
but no sound came from their mouths

riders from what barbarian past
from what barbarian future
their guns pointed
at our menfolk
at our boys

smoke and blood
and those we love falling
like little rag dolls
like the silence of the past
into words in a book
that we turn leaf by leaf
with heavy hands

the hands of women
from the barbaric past
putting out fires

the hands of women
from the barbaric future
covering the dead.

The Murdered Men
(to be spoken undramatically)

Levi Gates.
I lived a mile from town. At the sound of shooting I seized my rifle and went in. I fired two shots. Quantrill's men surrounded me. They shot me again and again. As I lay dead they beat my head to pieces.

George W. Bell, County Clerk.
I lived on a hill overlooking Lawrence. When I saw the raiders, I ran to warn the town. Too late. A man who often ate at my table promised to spare my life. He led me to his companions. They cried, "Shoot him. Shoot him." I asked for a moment to pray. Then four bullets entered my body.

Anthony Oldham, Black Preacher.
I was shot in the doorway of my house in the presence of my daughter.

Edward P. Fitch.
The raiders called for me. I went down and they shot me in the doorway. I fell down dead. They put six more bullets in my body and burned the house. My wife tried to pull me from the flames. They stopped her. She tried to stay in the burning house. They pushed her outside. One of them turned me over, took off my boots, put them on his own feet, and walked away.

Ralph C. Dix.
There were twenty of us inside the Johnson House Hotel. The raiders said if we surrendered we would not be hurt. They took us across the street to an alley and shot us all.

Old Uncle Frank, Runaway Slave.
I was ninety years old, heavy-set and lame. I hobbled away from the raiders. They shot me. I fell. Wounded, I lay still. Then I got up and tried to run. The raiders came after me. They shot me dead.

Mr. Burt.
I was standing in front of my house when a squad of raiders rode up and demanded my money. I handed it over. One of the raiders took it with one hand and shot me with the other.

Otis Lonley.
My wife and I were old. We lived a mile out of town in a little cottage. When the raiders came my wife pleaded that we cannot live long at the best. They shot me in my yard. I fell down, twitching. They shot me again and again until the twitching stopped.

George W. Collamore, Mayor.
When the raiders came to my front door, I slipped down a rope into the well in my backyard. As my house was burning, I heard my wife speak my name. I answered her. After the fire was finished, she came again to the well and called me. This time there was no answer.

Josiah C. Trask, Editor of the *State Journal*.
All four men in our house had weapons. When the raiders came I said it would be better for the town if we went with them. They marched us out of the house a dozen yards. While our wives looked on from the balcony, they shot us. One robbed my wife of her wedding ring. We lay in the sun half an hour. Another group came up and pumped more bullets into our bodies.

Judge Louis Carpenter.
I had been married less than a year. I spoke tactfully to the raiders. They left me unharmed, my house unburned. One asked where I was from. I said New York. He said people from New York are responsible for all the mischief. He shot me. Wounded, I ran to the cellar. He followed. I ran out into the yard. He shot me again. I fell. My young wife threw her body over mine. He raised her arm and pushed the revolver under it next to my head. My wife saw the bullet enter my brain.

Quantrill's Raiders

Early morning August 21, 1863
we rode into Lawrence
two hundred ninety-four men
four companies four abreast
William Quantrill on his great roan
Bill Todd Bill Anderson
Dick Yeager Frank James Jesse James
Jim Crow Chiles
silent in the dawn
like pages of history turning.

A yell a charge
down Massachusetts Street.
We shot people
where they stood on the road
firing into houses
shattering windows.

Smoke acrid powder
screaming and sobbing.

People fell
collapsed like rag dolls
filled with sawdust
seen from far away
from some barbarian past
falling into pages of a book
that turn leaf by leaf
like the cylinders
of our smoking revolvers.

Chorus

The sound of hooves
>   four abreast coming into Lawrence
>   riding down unarmed black recruits
>
>   through Massachusetts
>   through New Hampshire and Rhode Island
>
>   asking for men and boys
>   killing them where they stood
>
>   before the wide eyes of their families
>   between the outflung bodies of women

the sound of hooves
like rounds of ammunition
into the heads of the wounded
into the bodies of the dead.

The Uninvited

I came late
and sat silently
at the back of the room.

I have never entered your house
never met your children
        though their blood is mine.

Your births and your weddings
you celebrated without me.

I heard your music in the distance
and imagined your dancing
        your laughter.

Now you fall silent
as the priest enters.
He approaches the coffin.
You rise. I rise.

If I cannot share your joy
let me share your sorrow.

Part IV.

Lullabies

Music

An ancient instrument
        bone inlaid with gold
            ivory pegs for its vanished strings

            lies in an underground chamber
            at the foot of a silent prince.

And all around our home
as we lie in bed
on a dark night in late summer
        the rain has stopped.

A Dream of Old Classmates

The Alexander Ramsey House, St. Paul

August again 1961
early evening
under the elm trees

all my classmates
sit on the floor of an old house
huge as the elms.

Doc Whiting
long since dead
smiles as he calls roll
through his gray moustache
his bald head shining
like a streetlight:
        Dan Cashman . . .
        Betsy Edelson . . .
        Morris Edelson . . .
        Richard Halverson . . .
        Ed Ochester . . .
        Hugh Olmsted . . .
        Hertha Schulze . . .

The lights of the parlor
shine down
on their unmarked faces

as they sit on the polished wood floor
discussing the lesson for the day
        gesturing
          laughing softly
            talking in a steady hum.

Suddenly the big front door
swings silently open.

As if on cue
the class goes out.

Oh, no, says Doc, shaking his head.
Now they'll never come back.

I run out.
Wait! Come back! It isn't finished.

But already they are wandering off
in twos and threes
under the leaves and branches
of the huge elms
into the darkness

and only the crickets speak
under the streetlights

as I hurry back to the big house
of Alexander Ramsey
which is now dark and silent.

Lament for Water

Where have you vanished

    you
        that I found in stone
        that I took in my cupped hands
          to my face

Where have you vanished

Water

    pathfinder for my blood
    as it courses
        down the highway
          of my veins

Water

    in which my tongue moves

Water

    in which my eyes are set
        like onyx in silver

Water

    in which my hands are washed
        once again
          among the innocent

Water

    that nourished me
        in the womb

Water

    the last sacrament
    the last gift of earth

What is it
what is it
        comes floating silently

like a Lady of the Lake
        bearing a gift
                from another world . . .

Gravel at the Window

Listen: gravel
at the window

thrown long ago
far far away
across the sky

from the dark nebula
in Scorpius

the sound of the pebbles
dots and dashes of light.

Listen: the hushed whisper
of the calendar clock
in the next room

Come,
Share the night.

End of a Winter Evening

The door closes
thunt
like a book.

Out in the darkness
Pegasus gallops.

And the stars the stars
of the winter constellations
Auriga
Taurus
Orion

come down like good neighbors
to help push cars out of the snow.

Lullaby

Come away from the window
        come away
        come away.

The white frost
will do you harm.

Enchanted paths
        on the glass
will draw you from your home

into the world
into a mapless labyrinth
        a frozen land
                east of the sun
                west of the moon

where you will remain
caught
        in a web of frost

and never again
        never again

will you be warm.

Oranges

My old friend
sits with me a long table
filled with freshly cut oranges
      a cornucopia of oranges
        the air sweet with their smell.

We cup them in our hands
and sink our teeth in deep
deep down to the cores
the rinds against our lips
our noses wet with sticky sap

as the juice bursts in our mouths
      runs out over our lips
      runs down our chins.

More! More!
We devour them one after another
gorging ourselves as fast as we can
    like men working against the clock
    on a television game show
        drooling
        slurping
        laughing
    drunk on vitamin C
        we belch
        we burp.

And suddenly
we come at each other
squirting orange juice

like once we came at each other
with squirt guns aimed at crotches
      saying
          Whatsa matter guy
          kidney trouble?

laughing so hard
we can hardly stand

face to face
twisting oranges
into each other's mouths
noses eyes and hair

and then we are holding oranges
above each other's heads
      laughing
letting the juice drip down
      laughing and laughing
in little strange tongues
the way the Holy Ghost
descended on the Apostles

      laughing.

Memory

for Halka

She lives alone
somewhere
light-years away

weaving the night
with her long thin hands
under a white moon

cold as a frosty pump handle
cold as the iron chains
holding an empty swing board
in their arms

on an abandoned playground
in the blue night.

Dream Elegy

There we were at the great table
old friends reunited
laughing joking singing.

He lurched up from the table
to answer the phone
in the other room.
    I'll be right back.

Careful! Careful!
    we called above the music.

Then everything blurred.

Later
we found him unconscious
lying on an icy road
    his head tilted back
    a rock under his neck
    his legs splayed.

One took his head in both hands
two cradled his legs
two more on each side
we lifted him
    still warm and breathing.

We laid his body
    suddenly hard with rigor mortis
    and cold cold
        by the side of the road.

Unknown Insects

Your hand on my arm
we drift out
into the stellar sea
on the tide of our breathing.

The moon smears our windows
as if nobody lives here.

A lariat of stars
settles around the house.

The surreptitious gurgling
of unknown insects
in some far galaxy
travels clear and distinct
along the star lanes

as if they sang
right outside
on the lawn.

Gutters

All day the rain
has been coming down
and coming down

on the home
where my father
lived his quiet time.

I see him now
        coming
in the gray day
in his raincoat
        setting the old ladder firmly
        against the side of the house.

Up he goes
the ghost

a dead man
cleaning dead leaves
from the gutters

in the rain

his hands gentle and strong
doing
        what needs to be done.

Biology

The bell rings.

That's the end of English.
Books slam shut.
Papers ruffle.
The teacher turns away
and erases the blackboard.

Dave on my left
and Fred on my right
go out to biology.
Coming, asks Pat.

I put my notes
in my briefcase
and follow
down the pitted stone steps
across the mall

where the building
—what was its name?—
used to stand.

But it has vanished
along with Pat and Dave and Fred

and I am standing alone
a man of sixty years
with a high school biology textbook
long out of date

looking for my place
among the dead.

Keys

In my pockets
jingling like money
the keys
the magic keys

one by one
I touch them
carefully
as if they were alive

fit them into the locks
of the seven secret doors

and there
in the last room
where the old kings
kept their treasure

I find my friends
all of them
as if for a birthday party

their faces wrinkled
their hair gray
their hands held out
their hearts

those jingling keys
those magic doors
to the secret places
where I have spent my life.

Visitation

All right, Father,
put up your hands.

My old toy gun
with its rubber arrow
was trained on his ribs.

Slowly he lifted his arms
thin and stiff with age.
And the skin sagged
on the wrinkled face
I had touched so often.

Where are Barbie, Steph, and Tim?
We were supposed to go out and play.

—As if he would know,
that kind and gentle man
who had come back from the dead
to share my childhood

if only in dreams.

June

Slow . . . slow . . . slow.

Late afternoon.
Sun drowses on the horizon.

Cardinals trill *pedrillo, pedrillo.*
Orioles sway in the cherry boughs.

Red oak ash and locust
throw long shadows
over the lawn.

Little by little
dusk
turns on her lanterns.

Evening.

Pale friends
we thought long dead
return one by one.

And there, there
—just as we remember—
a thin summer moon glowing

and Ophiuchus
unrolling his dark cloak
over the growing corn.

Argo

Lo the great ship *Argo*
coming for us
bobbing through the clouds
on its long, long voyage

carrying star clusters
like heroes
sapphires and rubies
in her hold

floating on the foam
of galaxies

stardust in her wake

come now
to carry us away
from all that we know.

Homecoming

My business suddenly cancelled
my afternoon and evening
      unexpectedly free

and I am walking
up the railroad tracks
from Second Street

head down
plodding
one foot after the other
along the dusty wooden ties.

When I look up
I see it
the old house on Fifth Street
the Plymouth in the driveway
mother moving in the kitchen
father sitting at his desk
by the big window.

Slowly he gets up
opens the door
and comes outside

his eyes looking through me
      past me
down the road
searching for someone

as if I
were the ghost.

Somewhere Else

Somewhere else
I am walking
through piles of maple leaves

wading through a river
going back to my childhood

> father straight and tall
> his yellow lumberjack shirt
> his hair already gray

> mother planning and laughing
> reciting the magic words
> > *I think I can*
> > *I know I can*

> my little brother trying to keep up
> half running on his fat little legs

and all of us
walking through leaves
autumn after autumn
out into another life

as the leaves part before us
and follow in our wake
and rain down upon us
like blessings.

Black Stones

A man in darkness
dreams of stars

dreams
        hands outstretched
of feeling his way
        step by step
        up the dark marble
        of a narrow staircase

as I dip my right hand
thus

into a bowl
of black stones.

My fingers brush them
one by one

worry beads
beads of a rosary.

I will wash my hands,
I tell myself
among the innocent

as my white hand rises
like a shard of a moon
with two black stones

my gift to you
valentine

one for your left eye
one for your right.

White Stones

1
Little white stones
children in a walnut bowl

half moons of the fingernails
fingerprints of frost

core of the fruit
starpoints of light

fragments of the angel
who guarded paradise

with your round shoulders
your little pot bellies
and your long noses

hands have come
      to give you eyes
      to make you live.

2
At the dawn of time
you lay scattered like dice.

Priests saw in you
the will of the gods.

You came together
to make love
and discovered fire.

Placed on the tongue
you gave us speech.

You ward off witches
      diseases
      nightmares.

3
Come to me now
little brothers little sisters.

I will place you
at the crossroads of my life.

Take my hand.
Live.

Far Galaxy

Stars . . . stars . . .
as if by magic.

All of them strange.

Too many . . .
too bright . . .
too many blinking . . .

Where's Orion?
Polaris?
The northern horizon?

Flooded with light
we strain upward
open-mouthed
drinking in the sky

myriad points
lighthouses
fractured atoms

what we were
what we shall become

as neurons spark
and spark
and spark again
in some far galaxy.

Beyond Virgo

Stars stars
like drops of rain

and galaxies
spinning their stars
like children
in blindman's bluff

sending them off
on their little light legs
knapsacks on their backs
whistling
        through solar winds
         planetary nebula
        strands of dark matter

off to seek their fortunes
in the darkness and the light
      beyond Virgo.

Lamps

Dusk
comes down slowly
like the hand of a loved one
caressing your face
for the last time
and closing your eyes.

The lamps in our home
blink on
blink on
one by one

Stars
Light-years
and light-years
and light-years away.

The glass flowers of the lampshades close
and the glass birds seek out their night perches
in the fairy tale trees of the glass forest.

And there you are
in the big armchair in the corner

as you have been
year after year

reading by starlight.

A Day in Autumn

In the west
a fat moon
someone forgot
to turn off.

All day long
squirrels play
red-light green-light.

Bluejays call out
Ollie ollie oxen free!

A black cat
fresh from Halloween
bounds over the field
and into our arms.

Leaf by leaf
autumn
becomes transparent.

And there
at dusk
at the far edge
of the dusty playground

laughing
running with tiny steps
their arms full of leaves

we see our parents
        when they were small.

Acknowledgments

The author wishes to thank the following publications where some of these works first appeared: *Calaban, Epoch, 5 a.m., Forkroads, Hanging Loose, Kansas Quarterly, Kayak, Mr. Cogito, Naked Man, New Letters, Poets On, Poetry Now, Southern Poetry Review, Tellus,* and *Three Rivers Poetry Journal.*

"A Dream of Old Classmates" appeared in the anthology *Concert at Chopin's House* (New Rivers, 1987).

The author is grateful to the Hall Foundation of the University of Kansas for its support.

Victor Contoski was born in 1936 and grew up in the Polish-American community in northeast Minneapolis. He received his B.A. (ancient Greek) and M.A. (English) from the University of Minnesota. He then taught for three years in Poland. His wife Wieslawa is a native Pole.

He received his Ph.D. in American literature from the University of Wisconsin in 1969, and since then he has taught American literature and various poetry courses at the University of Kansas, where he was given the HOPE Award by the class of 2000 as the outstanding progressive educator.

He has written four books of poetry (two of them published by New Rivers Press) and three books of translations of contemporary Polish poetry. His poetry, translations, reviews, and critical articles have appeared in little magazines throughout the country and in many anthologies.

He won the fourth U.S. Postal Chess Championship.

His hobbies include classical music and looking out the window.